Becoming God's Masterpiece

By Balancing and Maintaining
Your Chakras through
Christ Consciousness

Written by Andrea Elizabeth
in Dubai, UAE

Copyright 2020 Andrea Elizabeth
This book is copyright under the Berne Convention.
All rights reserved.
No Reproduction without permission.
Printed in the United States of America
ISBN: 978-1-7346885-2-8
CATALOGING INFORMATION:
Elizabeth, Andrea
Becoming God's Masterpiece
By Balancing and Maintaining your Chakras Through Christ Consciousness
Filing categories:
OCC032000 BODY, MIND & SPIRIT/Angels & Spirit Guides
OCC011010 BODY, MIND & SPIRIT/Healing/Energy (Qi-gong, Reiki, Polarity)
OCC011020 BODY, MIND & SPIRIT/Healing/Prayer & Spiritual
BIO018000 BIOGRAPHY & AUTOBIOGRAPHY/Religious
SEL006000 SELF-HELP/Substance Abuse & Addictions/Alcohol
BIB020050 BIBLES/The Message/Study
Andrea's websites:
www.spiritualenergyhealingguide.com
www.beurownreligion.com
Facebook: www.facebook.com/andreaelizabeth2020
YouTube: www.youtube.com/channel/UCCX0V_sGJTh9wD-ZlA0WLPyA/featured?view_as=public
Patreon: www.patreon.com/AndreaElizabeth

Table of Contents

Introduction 1

Be Still and Know that I am God 2

Heaven Returns 7

The Seven Puzzle Pieces 9

God as Simple Grace 15

Interpreting God's Manifestations 16

Mantras of The Holy Christ Being 22

Day One, Chakra 1 25
Your Holy Altar of Christ
Defining your House

1st Chakra Mantra: I AM Holy 26

Day Two, Chakra 2 30
Your Holy Christ Being Reliance
7 Keys to Life in the Second Chakra

Day 3 Chakra 3 36
The Space of Your Sound Spectacularity
3rd Chakra Sallow or Belief
7 Keys to Life in the 3rd Chakra

Day 4 Chakra 4 43
The Chakra of Life
7 Keys to Existence in the 4th Chakra

Day 5 Chakra 5 46
Allowing God's Voice by Design
Finding Your Inner Voice Box
The Screaming OM

Day 6 Chakra 6 53
Clearing our Blind Spot
The Key to our Masterpiece

Day 7 Chakra 7 60
Our Crown of Divinity
The Flow of the 7th Chakra

7 New Fundamentals for Life 62

Chanting for Core Clearing 71

Toning for Core Clearing 73

Core Cleansing Chakra Chants 75

Core Cleansing Chakra Sounds of Love 77

Becoming God by Design 79

Ending Words 81

Introduction

I want to write this introduction to let you know that my writings are not at all like other writers. I write in a sort of communicative form with spirit, so my writings are a lot like questions and answers. I like to write in this form of communication so that each word or sound that is chosen, brings me a clear and concise working knowledge of what I am hearing, and so that it makes as much sense to the reader as to what is being said as I do not like to change the content much. So as you read on, you will begin to understand the format of my writings. I feel so compelled by spirit to get these words out to the world to form a community. I write for the greatest good of every single human and animal on this earth. I hope that what you read gives you that extra push to move up higher into a new realm of existence so that you too, can one day do this work like I do.

Blessings,

Andrea Elizabeth

Be Still and Know That I am God

These are the words I heard when I had the grandest epiphany of my life while in Dubai. For some reason this particular day I began asking about the shadow parts of me that I keep as a barrier to Christ. Then, it dawned on me, duh, this old-old prayer or religious saying or bible verse whatever it is states the full on answer to our being. To simply be still, and to know, that I -"I" am God. Holy hell, lol literally. My entire life I was taught to seek outside myself for God or a masterpiece of some sort, when I was the God I which I was to taught seek. Omg! I cannot even believe this right now!

I am fully exacerbated by all of this and I hope that you will be too.

As here as I sit writing in Dubai in the presence of Allah speaking through me, I begin shaking as I find out this insurmountable prevalent annunciation that hey everyone over here, I am God.

And what I find is when I am being God, and thinking God or God thinking through me, or allowing God to breathe through me, I am much easier to break through the old ideas and old promises I have broken to myself as not even having this understanding.

Here I sit as God living breathing crying and literally dying of the old person to whom I was.

I opulently derive my cataclysmic duties as Christ to bring to you this message of the Holy Christ being within.

As I am writing with this idea or feeling of homage to my patrons of art, I am now determined more than ever to show up and to be and to know in so many terms I live as though I am God or Allah. And in doing so I will no longer label it or him or her or them as a deity.

I will coinsure my life as a consummation of Christ which alternatively is God. I as God write these words in forms of books collections small issues, etc. as a part of who I am as a person living on this earth using the universal galaxy guardians as they are provided and assuredly helpful. The patron saints or even archangels are sort of chained or earthbound in assisting, but I have been given the knowledge that the guardians of the universe are not chained and can be more helpful. So, when we cry out for help begin using the universal assistance not the old dilapidated earthly existence. The earthly beings have limits on what they can assist us with but the universal guardians do not. I find it funny as I write this there have been movies about this guardians of the galaxy. Not exactly in God form but in assistance form, I believe therefore, breaking the delusion of no one out there to assist us.

They're there, they are just invisible and we cannot

know or see them until we are in such dire need of assistance. Which I feel sad because who can't always use a little help right

So I am asking Allah within as I write this the question.

Why cannot the own Holy man of his own peace and his own God's masterpiece see?

I think that is fair question?

Sure?

My dearest Allah Masterpiece, we all shall come forth to show how mighty one can be at any given time. When Allah is kept hidden in a dark market so to speak he sallows. In this sallowing Allah confines a deep mass or a deep crevasse of inner-turmoil and as much as this inner turmoil is most times the beginning place of some to cry out and call on Allah. This hidden space is mighty and can adhere to even a greater call. The call of your soul. Once your dear soul cries out from this hidden crevasse then the unimaginable takes place and Allah performs miracles in the eyes of the beholder. Others may not see the miracles, but the beholder can and will and does and then seemingly overnight they begin a new trek or a new life of believing in Allah.

Of course they seek first outside themself, as you have done, and if and when they have such a deep cleansing of ones souls space and find a new meaning of life to behold, then and only then can the magic be seen.

This is the Holy difference.

The Holy malevolence of man he keeps to himself. His malevolence is his downfall and he feels or finds it so very difficult to prevail given his past or his wickedness. He seemingly finds out that when once he has a boundless sense of Allah or God within he has a tantamount idea of whom he can become. But again as we all know one must die to live. And in the living the dying is a must. This is so profound and just that there always seems to be an unnoticed prayer to whom thine bounty shall remain. Here I giveth and here I taketh this is the primary idea of man.

In terms of malevolence he finds it uneasy to state that he has sinned or he has a malevolent space within him. However, at some point in the future, these deeds may break him down and force him to rely upon his own creator force within and this is where the truest of bounty lies.

Here is the majestic forest of his kingdom. Here is the breaking of the malevolence code for good. Herein lies creator force at its best when one is so down and so broken and so far away from his own self and knowingness this is the best time for Allah to appear and to behold. This is thy bounty in which we have heard of. Here is thine name and thine covenant. I shall become bestowed upon in the valley of the kingdom of heaven within and thus profoundly execute thine soul. The old presence is non sensical, and thine new presence is radical and profound as herein lies a pertinent value system of grace within and for the most part grace without. This is thy bounty as heaven awaits your return.

Heaven Returns

As I have written before heaven is the Holy reside within and it literally awaits everyone to who shall seek its return. The knowledge within our own soul's presence is an unwavering caprice or piece of fancy. It has its ups and downs and it has its primary job which is to show you how to live freely openly side by side with this delightful realm. Here we fashion the likeness of your soul to a say bell hop or front desk assistant I assure you it is so much more than that but I am in a hotel in Dubai and that is what coming to mind at this moment.

For the most part our soul reside is broken down into the particles or parts of an entire whole of a person. You fanatically deny this whole as your own whimsical fury waits for no one and you systematically are confined to a world or a desk or job of non-pleasure. You work un-pleasurably against your soul's purpose and to find ones soul purpose takes grace. From this grace one must commonly forget the old and commonly remember the new like, Oh yea, I am Christ, or I am God, or I am Allah. Constantly remembering is the most difficulty of it all. I find it so hard to remember, oh yea, I breathe Christ, I think Christ, and I love Christ. I consistently forget, but here I am today to help both you and I remember why we are Christ, why we are God and why we create light here now and forevermore in the hereafter if you so wish to so speculate.

I bring here to you on this day from Dubai a nation of one. A Holy empire as a spectacular commonality. I behold to you on this day of Holy matrimony a time-piece for your stature or prominence, distinction or standing. Whatever the case, I bring from my heart to you a place in which to carry out or fathom a constant meaning to God. In the times that one shall portray himself as a liar or a loser or adjunct to society this piece, or say missing piece of your puzzle shall be solved and remediated unto you by you.

Here are the methods I propose for your sanctimonious reside to begin to attain humility by and through each puzzle piece we find together. This a sort of treasure hunt for your soul. The pieces are even unaware they are hiding within so let's get started shall we?

The Seven Puzzle Pieces

❧

In Oriental Tradition 7 symbolizes individual soul. Together we will unfold the grandest nature of your soul.

Let's say there are 7 puzzle pieces beginning with your feet.

We will then begin working from your natural abilities by and through the bounty of your living conditions of your first Chakra. Here we are going to eliminate all dastardly deeds done both to you and by you so that you may find solace within your grounding chord to Allah.

Second, we will maneuver up to your second chakra ruminating ideas about how you got here in the first place. We shall rudimentary design a manageable space for you to unlearn old ideas about your past. Sexually, and eagerly see where your bias upon men and woman have taught you to live in separation. Thus creating a fortress of un-light within as to your sexuality, your imagination as well as your creative and artistic abilities. Who knew you had other crafts beside what you were so called trained to do and or become.

Third, we will concentration on your I AM status. Here we shall formulate and ponder ways to re-create a new version of your I AM presence. Here is your God center, your God consciousness as well as your human wisdom all balled into a crime area of alas blasphemy. This is commonly why the cry out for God is so very prevalent and rejoiced as this the real crime area of your life. Your human emotions have ruminated a blank or bland space into a total nightmare of a crime scene. Here is where you have formulated so much of your self-worth, your self-indignance, your self-reliance. All where you gave no one else a chance to assist you. You can do it all by yourself. And bam look where you ended up. Here reading this book of Creating God's Masterpiece.

Well first let me say welcome home my lovely friend. This is where the real rubber meets the road. This is the book of a lifetime, written, and channeled by God through God and for God that is the main resistance for most. One often thinks how you can say you are God when so many other Gods are out there and named already. And I say that is how and why you got here. We are mismanaged here on earth and in our lives to think that God is outside of us. An elongated version of a true hemisphere of worthiness that is only open to the ones of say richness beauty or glory. God in our eyes is glorified by beauty, yet if you look at the most God-conscious people from the past or present, the most are somewhat hideous and mainstay. Not to judge anyone, but to make a point. That God is not on the mantle or on the cross or on the golden statues

God is within you, in this third Chakra space in your living human body. That is the secret. We have never been told. So here we are going to represent God in terms of you. And you being God. And in this working book you are doing for God by God and with God in all ways possible. Singing God, loving God effacing old ideas of God as a deity. And re-living God as a possibility of his holiness of the creator, or creator God or simply grace. You can simply say I am grace and that pretty much sums it up. As God is grace and grace is God or so called. Anyway you have my point.

Forth stop, is going to make a hearty dependence on the Holy Christ being within. This diffidence space will utilize the grand fortress of your heart space. It will begin to illume your heart so as to fortify God's presence in each and every aspect of your being here you show just how silent you have been and how prevalent in man or nature you will become. This harrowing space of once controversial asylum will shatter or be shattered to become home to one and many who have not tried to find the difference between man and God, God and man, good and bad, right and wrong. Here we contemplate the fury of God's grace extemporaneously (spoken or done without preparation) but by virtue of silence. Here in silence we shall learn to contemplate light within so as you may provide others with said light.

Fifth, we shall combine all aspects of God or Gods voice here in your throat area and find the real reason you live. Do you live as to say creeping around at night in silence so as not to be seen or heard, or do you live in such a way that your voice is so loud that others cannot comprehend your volume. In short, here we shall begin to enunciate parts and beliefs of the old you. Here we shall reunify you with your voice self as god. Here we shall dignify your plight of love thy neighbor as thyself in terms of you literally being your neighbor without separation. And from here on out your life shall be lived in full unity and solace within so as to be lived in unity and solace without.

Now here are a few simple steps to form ideas as to your own passion.

1. What is your will to live?
2. How did you come about this?
3. What final choice did you have in taking on this role in your life?

Difficult questions to answer yet similarly comingled within the joys of laughter and speech and song and sound. All of these levels of groundedness are forms of unrelated bias's toward our self and others seemingly judging all day every day without coercion. We find it necessary to look at others and just to see where we stand in society, that we often times forget we are here and we become an unimaginable being so that is where this will be going.

Sixth, in terms of hiding of our past self, here this the litany of lies we have told, they are stationed right behind our third eye area and section of our brain.

Our knowingness is sort of defined by our bitterness, don't you think and our bitterness is ratified by our living, being and showing God to our self. Here we shall define once again how to form a true sense of knowing who I am. And why I am what I am.

However we shall partake in a form of self-adhesion or self-stricken or dubious ideas about who God was prior to now. I believe we have had some sort of lifetime in the past where we had a very strict adherence to praying to a God we did not like or understand, and then that lifetime was over. Now, once again we are here with this odd idea of God both inside and outside and we begin co-manufacturing ideas of how we even got here, who made you and why we are really living so unsatisfactorily. So for the most part this part will be adhering only to say past lives of us our forefathers and our makers our parents.

The well-wishers may have to sign off here, as it may get ugly... lol kidding it is part of this work that is truly needed as we need to aspire to succumb to the realization of who are we at our core being of our own core truth. It is fathomable or unimaginable. There may be two due courses to take but this will be the easier way. So we will begin in a timeline of the past when God created us. This is the beginning when we were told, but how can that be when we know there is more?

Finally, at the 7th realm of existence we shall embody Christ or Allah as you have come to know him or it by now. We shall together solidly state a phenomenal prayer of hope and forgiveness and living a true nature of God or Christ or Allah in one super being of God. I in thee and thee in thou. We are all in one capacity to live to love and to behold God's grace within. This is the past masters dream for you. To have absolutely every single living being attuned to the greatness of one's soul. God's masterpiece all sectioned out for you to examine and even portray if you so shall wish.

At this point, I am inserting here a portion of my 21 day book, called What If You Were God? As I believe the explanation I received is latent and just.

God As Simple Grace

So for the most part, we are designed to be a symbol of the grandness of the light, which to me is simple grace, a God-given right or apathy of a design from the wisdom of the universe, maybe from the heavens or from the Gods. Grace originated somewhere deep within the conjecture of God; somewhere in man and somewhere in our soul and its creations are also within the sun and the moon. At the very time of our creation, there was a sudden spark, a sound, a light, a resonance and boom! — Our grace was born as we were born. Yet, somewhere, some of us have forgotten that we are born of grace, we are born of love, and we are born of forgiveness. We slather on layers of paint or other versions of self at times so as to not be able to vibrate the resonance of grace, because we feel at times we are so unworthy.

Reading about God as if He is a man has many difficulties for some, as most people have been taught that God is something outside of themselves to pray to or honor.

I do believe we have been taught the opposite as I believe that we are all God inside or at best, vibration ally and that we can begin to change our thoughts on this and live as though we are God.

Not God in terms of a Deity or as one to Behold, but I have been told to give the God name of thinking in terms of vibration. The term I have been told to give it is the Holy Christ Being (HCB) the unnamed literal hunt for this vibration. Whatever works for you. Make this idea something that you can trust and understand. As I am typing this, I am seeing a golden being or golden light as I say the words Christ or Christ being. Also, as I am typing this, I am allowing the heavens above to ruminate light for all who are reading this book. I give to you on this particular day a look back into the time when our own religion kept you or us in the gallows of hate. So I take you back even further into our galaxy explosion or expansion or birthing. Whatever we were, we were the idea of what was to come, and there was a vibration, or a vibrational pull, or a tug somewhere universally. That is what I am being told, and now I believe, and I have been told this is the very beginning of the Holy Christ Being of light. This light, this sound, this vision of life came from somewhere. Not from man as man himself is disharmony, but the Christ light or Christ Light Being is harmony. Literal Perfection.

The idea of the Holy Christ Being forming as, a song for our life is magnificent and this song is our own version of the Holy Christ being Magnificence in each of us.

We can all speculate here and there what really

happened before we were alive. But for reduction of discussion, lets all agree that something happened out in space in the universal grid or matrix of our mere beginnings. And if you think about it as the universe, all things of matter are specific to the resonance or ratio of Pi, which is a mathematical calculation by man, of course, to signify perfection. And I believe this. Mostly because Sir Isaac Newton, Einstein, Aristotle, Plato as well as Pythagoras have given me the opportunity to hear their words and write with and through them about this universal vibration and how it applies to man.

In terms of Universal Vibration, I do not believe these men come to me as men alive, I believe that I somehow tapped into their own benevolence and their own fragment of themselves as a vibration. As the universe speaks in vibrational resonance, I believe so do they. Which is why I believe I am able to hear them. Hang on, it's going to be a bumpy ride. Blessed be to all and may to come.

Interpreting God's Manifestations
❧

Learning to interpret God's manifestations quickly in our lives in so as to being a capitulated being of sight. Once a day remind yourself here to fathom and or understandingly give your self-aspect over to the Holy Christ aspect of your being. Here you are Be-ing God itself. Or being a God. Here you begin to wonder, fathom or even ascertain a new value to your once undervalued self. Here you quickly and arguable define who what and where you stand today now. All else is out the window.

We are now, creating a prism of God in God and for God – ME, or YOU.

Here we find indelibly that our creative force within has a giant ego which needs smashing. And here with this workbook of findings of our own God within us we will indelibly know who we finally are. All those questions are finally going to be answered and we here together co-create answers to our age old seeking as to who God is and why he was lost or adversely and or profoundly misplaced.

Here we find that looking so deeply within our soul of manna, here today we co-create a vision for our life together. You are not working alone here, let me first say that. There are hundreds of thousands and a multitude of grace beings surrounding us, this planet and the universe now today as we speak and read these quarrels of harrowing facets of self within. Here we find that hundreds of thousands of allies are sitting on the edge of the moon sort of signaling our existence. But, how many actually even look up and away from our capitulated self? A self of a relegated existence.

Here on earth we find or think it privy to only those on some type of higher given title or sense of intelligent existence more than we have. We all seem to think of someone has more money, or is more educated or is somehow a movie start or actor, they seem to fall into Gods graces. Here on this planet I can assure we are the only species to find this indelible. On this planet we sanctify beauty as a mark or sign of intelligence and or candor however as we who have lived some years here, we all find that not so. So as I sit here in Toronto Canada and finish writing the open book which began in Dubai, I find it very necessary to ensure each of you that all one needs to be privy to is what equation or finesse do you wish to endure? What is the most intense pain you have gone through in order to seek this God or your blatant misunderstanding. Here we find a necessary say evil of both the two worlds in which we live.

Once we keep being hounded by the endless marketing of the beautiful people here in our world to market products that we l think will make us look beautiful like the famous and yet we keep playing into this marketing and find our lives are still yet unfulfilled. The marketed items are for the elite and the expense of all of it very great and some people honestly go bankrupt financially as well as spiritually trying to chase that fix of beauty.

Eagerly to behold a grand version of their lives which seemingly is unfulfilled and rather dull. So to save the expense of the rational of say haste I now give to you the unsung song of Christ as a song within. Here we find it very necessary to unfold each layer of our skin or soul, layer by layer to provide to us the untold story of our soul life. Yes we have lived here for so many years in this life but, how can you begin to fathom the total upkeep of your mantra well within the confines of your soul space and how can you begin to ascertain its value.

Here the most undervalued vision for our soul space is the character in which we strive to live. Here we find it sometimes necessary to sell little parts of our soul for this or that, or to get this or become that and so here we find it very necessary to begin there in that space of underdeveloped chicanery. In this space we come and go as we please and we underdeveloped our case of say wine or berries. Here we have a full-fledged garden of our soul in which to pick and choose from, yet we only pick the wonders of what we think the world out there wishes for us to proclaim as us. We undervalue all other parts of who we are

and from a distance we intermittently find a piece of likening to us. as sometimes we may see a forest of trees where the light opens up and you can seemingly and or profoundly think now there is God, in that light above those trees and then you inadvertently and or seemingly just go on about your business, never really pondering who or what the meaning of that exact thought really is or is privy to. here we conjoin two worlds as one and we never really find the full true meaning of our existence here on this planet and here we also find that our conjoining factors of say life and death play a full on role to society as they also market the wares or goods to keep us all on a fear based life. If you don't buy this cream, you will be ugly and then you shall die ugly. Lol well not exactly like that, but the consumers feel this way. If you are not beautiful and rich and have lots of money you shall not be free, you shall be kept in the ugly garden locked way
from freedom.

All in all we shall begin to portray a vision for your soul's space to reside. Here you shall keep up the heavenly garden of self. Here we shall omit the ugliness and begin profoundly dreaming in our beauty of Christ, here are the beauty of kindness of God's words.

Mantras of the Holy Christ Being

Here in our First Chakra is where we begin to grow our self into a mantra of or for the Holy Christ being. This is where we find happiness, solitude and grandeur all well within our wholeness to love and to keep loving. This is where our soul remains hidden in the atrocities of this space nation of one as a placated vision of health. How healthy is our soul. Our manna has to be greatly provided for in terms of healthy light love and relegated terms of hospice. We are literally dying in this world of hatred and such. Here we find it very necessary to remedy our soul's space for a time of peace. Here we can almost foresee a sense of homage or duty to all to whom have fled the scene here, their souls could not take it. And it seems that checking out was the only why home for these souls. Just because they checked out, does not render them bad or good, it just renders them safe. Here on this lancet the source of human indignity and human massacre at levels not even known here to man on this planet, as there are still forces of slavery in so many facets that we don't even realize. Today we are still slaves to society's rules and the rule makers who indelibly can give a rat's ass about any of us to whom they do not socialize with and yet, they are leaders of our planet. So socially we cantor to their homilies without grace and doubt of our soul's existence. Here is an inferno just socially waiting to erupt and this planet is going to dust. So what can any of us do about it? Well I believe that first we shall all take a look at what fully shaped us as an individuals, and then perhaps as a whole society, as in another book I shall write. Well, I guess I shall be wring more than this book. For starters.

We shall begin here today with a full on magnificence of God extravaganza and add heaping spoonful's of love light and extraordinary magnificence. Here we begin our journey deeply within and with a fortitude of great manga carta to look here we find exactly how when and why we falter so deeply within our soul center. We shall place a sallow of hope into our remaining spectacularity and find our own wherewithal in and throughout our secessions. Here we shall begin the unknowing fallacy of say great Brittan as we are such an island of primeval relics and ways and hindered God seeds. We shall under ways in which to opulently remain as teachable as possible in order to find our soul or our souls reside. Here we find it so very necessary to undo the past and to remain fully in an opulent position of Christ where we each stand individually as well as conglomerately as one being of God or Christ or grace.

Each step up into your temple shall give way to the meaning of Christ I am. Each remnant of past self-dissuasion created shall be recreated with a new version of the Holy Christ being within and therefore shall remain stable and fulfilled in and throughout this souls presence and this souls life here on this planet.

There shall be no longer an atrophied soul reside it shall be a congress of a multifaceted Christ within. As though you are seeing yourself as a stained glass window with all facets of Christ as the sun shines through beaming its light through each and every soul window, shall a sallow of a beam of light behold and there shall openly and creatively be light within that light and co-create a beam of sanctity and wholeness abound. Here is your soul song, here is your soul remembrance here is your soul light. Lit well within your own soul crevasse. Here is where the sound and song begins; within your magnificence of God; your creation your relation to and your vibration of it. A soul creative force of God's magnificence. And so shall we begin.

Day One • Chakra 1

Your Holy Altar of Christ

Becoming a Christ being brings the greatest of gifts to all and it benefits well to whom shall cross your path and it shall become a soul congruent labyrinth of Christ. Here your soul shall begin Christ residing or a Christ residence. Hereto shall lie a grand and formidable secret room or secret space where you can souly remember your cadence as well as your forthwith to homage? Here you remain seated and grounded and live fully home, within. Here are your remnants of holiness.

Defining your House

The 1st Chakra remains hidden for so many ideas of Christ. Here as we sit and perform our homage to our self as say queen, king or apostle for a day or forever we relegate never again. We pay specific homage to us as or in a form of Holy be thy name. I am forever in a space of non-relegation ever again. I sit Holy, I feel Holy, I am Holy. This is a good mantra to use for this 1st Chakra work

1st Chakra Mantra: I AM Holy

This keeps us in a frame of mind or within the mindset of Christ forevermore in our soul's space. This master symbolism remains true to form of this house is a Holy house therefore, I reside, and therefore, I live. Holy! Wholly! I love this. I live! Period. Nothing more to say, nothing more to give, insight into, simply I live. I am Holy; therefore I live, Holy!

Now in coveting this statement we give treatment or homage to our soul by stating that I am Holy therefore I live. How does that feel when you read it? I am Holy; therefore I live. This simple statement really gives the old life a run for the money. Therefore, we shall begin to pacify our soul.

How can someone like me say these words yet feel unadulterated and sound? This is the work we are sharing together as the old remnants of our broken soul space remain hidden, they will keep our foundry brittle, so as we work through these energy centers of our soul body space we shall keep shattering the old and placating its space as to forming a new bond or foundational resonance of peace and sheer joy.

And as we manufacture grace we manufacture joy. Here we have managed to placate your body space as a form of undoing the nature of man and redefining the nature of God in your soul. This souls space has and forever shall be sacred and how can it not be sacred as you follow Christ and in its beginning you sallow the unburden of wholeness, you simply got led astray and got lost. The trail up to now has been stricken from your soul as to terminate the old and replace with the new. Abound we go now.

1st Chakra Mantra:

> *I am Holy;*
> *therefore I live.*

Now these statements are as multifaceted as to how your soul shall manage the remaining 6 Chakra workings. Each placated space shall inform the relegated that I am Holy; therefore I live and then in terms of say block building we shall form a talon of grace and eliminate all other resides or residual deformities. Herein lies the depths of one's true manna of and for God itself a true relegated dismissal of the old and a true form of life or light for a core of pure goodness and light. This form of blocking is showing one how to be stable and true

Here are some forms of truth for your survival...

- ◊ A new soul revival is our soul truths or privities.
- ◊ Create a new bond with your force while still needing attention.
- ◊ Keep your force within your truest of honor space.
- ◊ Eliminate all aspect of Un-Holy.
- ◊ Remain teachable and re-trainable.
- ◊ Keep a sheer knowledge of your truth. Who am I?
- ◊ Whenever I shall falter back, I shall get my sheer footing once again.
- ◊ There are no losers - only beginners as each beginner fully becomes their own leader.
- ◊ Within is in!

For each of these types of hindrances, which keeps us most eluded?

How can and will you remain inside when any of these typical efficacies show up?

Using the mantra is key here that way we no longer affiliate with each eroding idea or though or manifestation of our past self. Here we manage to follow each step fully and retrain our minds into a form of self-reliance and begin to pick up our own sheer footing and move on toward keeping our feet firm and planted well within our channel of God.

I am Holy;

therefore I live.

Day Two • Chakra 2

Your Holy Christ Be-ing Reliance

In keeping with the Holy mantra for the 1st Chakra we shall now align with our new foundation. Herein lies our truth of our causation of our Holy Christ Be-ing's reliance. First we replace our home foundational refuge and now secondly we relegate its old existence or our old thoughts of our creation or creativity space.

We now remain teachable as to our creativity, our co-examination and our livelihood. For many this space here is a blocked cavern of self-doubt and self-hatred at times

We establish from a very young age, how a stomach ache keeps us from having to do many a thing. Her we find it almost formidable that once as a child seeks astonishment, there can be a boundless use for this Chakra space as here we find necessary accomplishment, yet extraordinary un-accomplishment as so many have shut off this beautiful creative space in their lives as a sort of self-punishment for all. As if I shut down my creative forces the ones who have hurt or even forbade me of being who I am in so many sorts of ways shall suffer and they shall never see my plight of my existence.

My grandeur, my light, my sonnet, my God. Here is the real black op if you will, this is significantly more than just a space for say existence or birth or creating. This is the space of where the real mother of pearl resides. Here is a grand manufacturing space for and of our true light so shine and or to cover, which may have been the case. Once we show and uncover your Be-ing-ness you shall shine once again and you shall never be the same as you once were. You shall shine and out shadow your remaining hidden relegated shore or embodiment. Your lapse in time of having this part of you outshine the rest is now going to be so very prevalent in your manner of living that you shall portray like no others before you or even after you. You shall flourish in the sheer manner of love they neighbor as thyself so in terms of hallowed indictment you shall be living form a signage of here I am – I am God-hear me roar-see my sign-give me hope allow my light to show and to shine and to thrive well within the flurry of life or Christ and hurry me up to know this as I am and shall forever be in the Holy mercy of the Holy Christ beings here I reside and pay full homage here within and the flurries of life shall begin to rise up and above my old sallow of withheld living. I shall forevermore be boundless and free living in an insurmountable aspect of God. For it is here that I shall remain full or full on teachable in my old faltering ways, out with the old and in with the new; remembering that I am Christ within this is my second Holy mantra.

2nd Chakra Mantra:

I am Christ within, therefore I shine

The atrocities of man or society shall never again lull me down into the pits of despair or injustice; I win therefore I live. Life is just a simple everyday monotonous fury of hate and as I strongly disagree with the old, I shall reinvent with anew I am here to amplify my own relevance and piece together my own soul light as to create a lit sensation of home or homage. I shine, there I live. This too is a primitive light adjustment. As soon as we state this, we reinvent our will. Many a time when we do things against our wishes or our will because of a parent or we wish to please someone regardless of how it affects us, we go against all aspects of our true self and therefore our soul reside diminishes a bit. So in each of these next relefied statements we shall imagine that only we are Holy and only we shine. We are gathering truths of our soul in order to really indemnify or ratify our significance deep within our 2nd Chakra and create from a place of light love and endearment of our own soul life. We have never before actually even given thought to this soul life and have allowed it to be squandered about like little snowflakes on the driven snow we simply allowed each piece of our manna to dismember our light and little by little we remained dark and dim in our soul space and our fevered for life became limited. So with each imaginal gift here we find a new sort of creation for our soul space and the sully is past and the remnants are new. So here give your soul the gift of life. Remaining teachable is the key here.

7 Keys to life in the Second Chakra

Here we agree to select a few of God's life-giving creations, feel free to engage within and ask for more if you so shall require. There are so many keys to finding your soul, so, here, imagine only the specific ones that relate directly to you. Each perspective is quite an honor; see to it that each heart thought is identified souly. Perform your soul duties as perfection. Here you shall march upon the wonders of creation; become laden with the force of intelligence as herein lies the co-creative remnants you so shall seek.

- ◊ Your perfection is wisdom that comes from within.
- ◊ Living forever in the soul reside, for it shall bequeath to you an astonishing remembrance of home.
- ◊ This shall also bequeath to you an insurmountable talent for homage inasmuch as you shall be provided light.
- ◊ The quickening of your soul's light has power in your wisdom.

◊ Herein lies a wealth of astounding gifts to do insurmountable things. Forget this not as this is your bounty.

◊ Step deeply into this 2nd Chakra work for fun. It is an indelible space for a delightful shanty. Thus shall remain in deep proclamation of home.

◊ Therefore, living free and open and in Gods reside within this 2nd Chakra space is they master key to alignment and precisely the way to proceed into the Chakra number 3 as this house is where the fun truly begins.

Day Three • Chakra 3

The Space of Your Sound Spectacularity

    Chakra 3 or the hara between 3rd and 2nd Chakras space is a sound spectacularity for homage. This magnificent feat is one of dramatic and sound environment to become fully established by some. And hopefully you. Herein lies a kindness so deeply engrained into every ounce of our makeup of God that we sometimes are played the fool by this space as our soul's kindness will keep taking in the foolishness of others time and time again because we are so free in this soul space.

    We kindly give and give and give and the takers take and take an take and we are provided a listless amount of grand forbidy likening to a pail of untethered bound love; the sea of love here is a boundless sea of empathy and many are taken advantage of because of it... so this is a very kind yet manipulatable space. So we shall relegate the say unruly part of this say misgivings and get to the real interior meaning of this space and to its goodness or God-ness here we shall formally provide for you a space of homage by simply realigning the following design.

Designing your Intuition Space

When in doubt in this gut space allow the emotions to be followed all the way through to the end. This is the empathy we all develop as children and we seemingly never really force our way into needing to change anything else about his space except when we formally do not signify a great amount of bliss as say when we see a little baby or puppy. We can always find that in our 3rd Chakra space we formally see the absolute good in all things. And because of this goodness space we seemingly and sometimes profoundly dismiss the bad in others. I for some reason cannot seem to place a bad bone in anyone and I am reminded all the time by my family about this. Because I feel everyone is good, regardless of what has been said or done... now as much as this is entirely a good thing, it could be bad in some situations as to as say a robbery or a plight of self-destruction. Like even though we know that eating an entire chocolate cake is bad we do it anyway and find the later consequence to be enough to bring down a bull. So to speak. We often forage past that small voice and do not head or own call if you will. That 3rd Chakra has a sheer mind of its own and we oftentimes relinquish it as an undetermined space and then after the fact often feel misguided and often times underachieved. We minimize our say foraging space and forge into head understanding. So where we shall remain in the 3rd Chakra space and give to you some real food for thought. As it has been said that our guts have a mind of their own and forsaking them for just am moment can lead us into deep dark territory and for the most part relinquished beyond measure. As it seems we are never taught to trust our gut and at many levels at many times we do not and get into heaps of trouble and often ties we find our self in a dark place spiritually emotionally and even physically all by not just listening to our inside voice. I found this out myself and at one point mismanaged my life almost beyond repair at some points, which as lead to here to writing this book of the prophets. You didn't think I was doing any of this on my own did you. By all means no, I am guided to sit and to write by channeling these words as exact as I can manage. And if I have the incorrect word coming in I will be stopped until the correct word comes I and I type it. Some of this takes a while as some of the words coming through do not seem right or appropriate, I have to stop and look these words up in the dictionary as I have absolutely no idea as to some or even most of the big words used in my writings. This information I channel I believe comes from a deep source in the universal mind and I fully attribute this God given task to my work as paralegal, and a spiritual teacher. I believe both have assisted me at times on my spiritual journey as I have had to deeply go inside my own soul so many many times to find answers because the world I was seeing on the outside through my own eyes made absolutely no sense, but as I was guided to use my gut more and more, I began to see the earnest ideas and the teachings and lessons I was to laden with. And in my profession as both of these I kind of went off the grid and began to write from home and in this capacity I am gaining a new even higher perspective of God within as I am most quietly and wear earplugs. I force out the living world and work within my human spirit world using mostly techniques from my life which entertain new found ideas, feelings, moods and homage to God within. This sitting business however has made my bottom grow a bit, but I am ok with that... I would much rather sit and meditate with my God inside than openly go out into the world of turmoil and noise. I rather love my silence and my retreat within.

If anyone would ask me what I love to do most, I would answer siting and conversating with my God within, as it feels fantastic as this interdependent presence allows for me to feel comfortable and engaging well within my own sprit and be, I rather adore my soul space and the feelings of this presence within. I feel whole, fully capable of so many things and ideas and as I fully eliminate all outer world presence and sound and I souly feel gifted into my own sound or song resonance within and I truly and deeply know myself a full capacitor level of grace and steed. I am fully alive, I am whole I am fully present and I can attribute all of this to my stationary space and yes fuller bottom I love sitting in this souly quiet space and putting my reference or my intelligence space or mind's eye space in my 3rd Chakra space. From this space, I indelibly receive pleasure as I assist the rest of my soul space to continually rely on this space and not my brain. The more I sit with my focus upon this 3rd Chakra space or hara space I am fully recognize as me and this allows me to fully function as me for me and by me. I no longer need outside recognition explaining me to me. I know me, I feel me, and I love me. This is the lesson from this 3rd Chakra work I adore me. I love me and I honor me. This way I can no longer allow others to not honor me. In whichever way they feel either threatened or uncomfortable. I shout myself as God out loud as best as I can to fully articulate me. I am me in this space as full on as honest and as remnants of Christ, sort of like that stained glass window in the previous chapter. I reside in God and God resides in me. I am fully and resonating deeply within the soul creation space of God and me as we. Here I find it incredibly sufficient as to needing anything more to fulfil my life any further. I feel sufficient and full and whole. What more could one want. If I were to never need to have outside sources to live, say food, shelter, etc., I would simply sit each day in this Holy remnant space of Christ and breathe in the power of God and exhale the power of God. Fully simply and forever I honestly feel I have no other wants than to want to sit here in this God space and be and for the record, this is the exact space I am writing from and I believe that as God you are receiving this goodness as I am portraying and hoping that you are receiving this message so that you too can find this God inside and live in nirvana so from this idea lets see that we shall be doing for this third Chakra space work

First of all we shall always remember that God and I are one and that all aspects of goodness are I as well as when the dawn breaks tomorrow my brothers and sisters of God shall rejoice in their own God by fully emancipating their own dawn as a tribute to the fallen. And as each person find their own nirvana as their dawning arises so shall you find the remnants of your past lives and they shall whisper into your shadow self and remediate your soul space into a dream life presence.

Here shall we begin.

3rd Chakra Belief
7 Keys to Life in the 3rd Chakra

Allow the Holy Christ being to become alive and well within your dream like state- nirvana is life

- Co create a life where all are one and equal
- Furnish our planet with goodness and love for life by allowing your soul's nirvana to be fertile with joy
- Live in and from a nature of plight for love as love conquers all to whom this is not their light
- Live life, enjoy life, bring life
- However honest thy shall become, become souly bound by honoring your soul; here is your key
- Master your key and therefore master your God self as herein lies the kingdom of heaven
- Nirvana and heaven are aligned here in your soul space

Day Four • Chakra 4

The Chakra of Life

Here we ascertain a sort of co-creative space where yoHere we ascertain a sort of co-creative space where you are in alignment with the holiest of mantras within. Thee in though, and though in thee.

A sort of magical defiance to the world; that so many have been taught that their book is the one and only book of God and for so many was the only way to our heart space. Now I am writing this in a sort of foretold version of the only Holy manna known to man is so deep within he or his heart space and the relegated past religionist seemingly saw to it that most past religions seem to preach of an outer God and not a heart space God. So I am not here to say everything is wrong, I am just here to say what I am hearing to channel is not right or wrong, but informative. So I bring to you an informative sight on God in our heart and in our 4th Chakra. I also adhere to a kind loving space for us all as Holy Christ Beings

Our 4th Chakra energy center of the heart has a magic all of its own. It manufactures light and imagery galore. It co creates a cycle of fantasy for some but for others it magnifies their existence. As there have been images of the heart creating a torus of light this space I believe our heart magnifies our truest of existence and begins the path of our glory. Here we find it culturally significant that each person knows that the heart signifies love and love signifies the heart. And there is magic in knowing this as from one's heart our glory states firmly and deeply that this is my residence and that I shall not have to falter because of it. So many people live from a place of a broken heart and know not of this presence. Here one can adhere a space full of a litany of Christ homages yet still be unfulfilled in their life. Here we seek to feel rather than to know. If we are suffering from a broken heart area we are unfulfilled to say the least and we are broken into tiny little fragmented piece of doubt. And in this doubt we never fully seem to recover fully until we find the light of our heart inside our soul and come to realize that our soul is God and God is our soul. So from this 4th Chakra work we identify 4 things in which to contemplate for your spiritual heart growth.

How many more times shall you endure pain from others to whom have no known knowledge to one's soul?

How can you re-live the pain over and over again if How can you re-live the pain over and over again if you have found your God within your soul space? This litany of pain is now overturned and you have remedied your past broken heart space with each and every person, idea, place, man, women, child, every single thing that kept you in pain is now relived as you can now know in your heart space is the residence of God and in this space of God pain is a nonresident. In living in nirvana and heaven no hell exists for you any longer; you are relieved.

Which way is up? So to speak, or in herein lies your bounty; remember you are God

Behold in the unilateral existence is pain, but in the co-creative existence within you all pain subsided and you exist only in light and love.

The Seven Keys to Existence in the 4th Chakra

◊ God realm not self-realm.

◊ God existence is maintained within fully.

◊ Your capacity to align within comes as naturally as your breathe; breathe in with God, and breathe out with God; this is the flow of magnificence.

◊ I am creator God within; no furies exist; only peace and calm within.

◊ Inside lies my bounty and therefore - my magnificence.

◊ Herein lies Gods truest magnificence; I in thee and thee in thou.

◊ All my past plights are over now; the living shall begin.

Day Five • Chakra 5

Allowing God's Voice by Design

Here in this specialty energy center we endure such a mockup of heretic sometimes we energetically find that passages of our creator seemingly coming in and out of our voice space coincidedly rendering our God space Holy and free from Holy manna from heaven and at other times we meandering in a space of resistance so as to form a God unrelated vision for our home.

As I write this piece for a sort non solution space I can only surmise that here I write in a sort of a blurred vision only to use my voice as my sight. Here I gain a new perspective of harmony as to the absolute truth of my story of my light. Our light is truthfully gained or ascertained as a sort of resembles of our own Holy container and in this is Holy container we find that our own spiritual wellbeing is sometimes attacked even by our own self. Now really think about the ideas that run through your consciousness about you and yourself and even your God if we were to ever question that. How do these words seemingly feel in your harnessed voice of self? Has your voice been captured by others has your voice been thrown away by various corporations or unvalued as a human being. How many times have you been shut down as to your song of life? How has your heaven begun to show itself and then been annihilated by someone's words or actions. We find it sometimes difficult especially if we are empathic or adversely complicated and or sensitive to really find our voice at times when we really, really, need to find it. And it is in those times of need of our how heavenly self that we became shunned or annealed to a deep degree of non-homage and found no place within to seek shelter. So in other ways we found it necessary to deliver our plight of love as a say misogynist or sexual atrophied being. We became insightful, yet unrelatable to so many as we were contaminated by what others had said and done to us. We shut off completely and irrationally and never really endeavored our way back into our say societal voice or even our voice of heaven so what we shall be delivering here in this 5th Chakra work is finding our way back home for the holidays within and finding our own natural sense of God in our voice. And literally honing in on the injustice of our capitalization of our truth of our calling.

Here we provide a way in and through to our soul where we can escape our facade we have created and truly be relieved of our capers. We have an illusion that once we have found our soul at our deepest level, there shall be no more intrusionary aligning, but the fact is that there is still much more to do around this magical voice endeavor and you in particular are going to be astounded as to how much more strength you can carry around within your say voice box and really begin to ascertain a new variance in your say human form or your past illusory song.

Here we banish your old sound and co-create as well as co-mingle your plight. As our plight is your plight and your plight is our plight. So your soul remnant space of song has its own harmony and delightful state of grandeur and by allowing your song to virtually be heard from your own truth you shall regain your own inner power your own inner magnificence and your own inner Be-ing. You will Be seen, and you will Be heard and you will Be loved. All by you. Remember we no longer seek for privilege out beyond our own self, we continually only seek inward as a way of mastery and a way of keeping our own fortune. As the more you coincide with what others think of you or what they say to you , you give away some of your fortune. A fortune in which you worked very hard for and is every bit yours. When you turn away for knowing that you are God and you indelibly offer your thoughts or ideas to what the media says you should look like or what your mother tells you what you should accomplish, bye bye, goes your fortune you have worked so hard for. So from now on eyes inward, not outward and by all means do not allow heaven to be manipulated by anything or anyone. You are extraordinary in every single way. Now let us get to work

Finding Your Inner Voice Box

Your voice has some hearts strings which have gut strings, which have creation strings which have homage strings. All which play their part in co-creating your voice box so to speak and from this voice box we inevitably co create manna from heaven.

How well do you know your own voice? And if you were to hear it fully and clearly would you even begin to imagine it to be you or yours? How well do you know what it is about your voice that keeps you lessened? And in what terms have you shut it down? Now these are important questions and as assuredly they each have relevant answers. You may wonder about them or dramatically wash them away. As we have cleared the space in this Chakra, you may endure your own feverishly relevant gasp of fresh air once and for all as we are all relatively certain that at some point in your heaven space you shall prevail quickly from a space of enduring light.

Your own forbidden seal must be broken and displayed or the world to see and you shall become free from your own past horrors of non-speaking or voicing your own opinion.

We have covered quite a few offerings, let's allow for the rest to be supplied

Now can and will you offer up your own free speech? Do you have any awareness of what this free speech could be?

For instance how many times and in what fashions

have your voice been soberly and or very quickly cut off. Be it a friend, a colleague a parent a sibling; and in this how did you feel individually? Did you feel lost or betrayed or both?

And having been preyed upon in your life how would it feel to be openly free from any of that at all? Living in a space of I am not going back to the space ever again and I am never having to relive those feelings again.

Well I would hope that you would agreeably say yes that you would like to be free from the inadvertent shut down and labored pain which has caused your voice to shut off and be unaccounted for. So here I add a great solution.

The Screaming OM

With this sustained idea in mind we shall recomm-mWith this sustained idea in mind we shall recommend that you find a most turbulent aspect of idea that you have of your own self because of this get really fired up about it. Allow all of the emotions to well up into your voice and begin to bring the fire from that emotion into your voice box and allow yourself to literally scream it out. Scream it out as many times as you need to so that you voice box becomes a freedom box. Do this so many times that you are tired of screaming. And when you have become tired of this screaming, I want you to take a deep breath and OM from your 1st Chakra to your 2nd Chakra to your 3rd

Chakra to your 4th Chakra to your 5th Chakra. Just like DO, RE, MI, FA, SO----OMMMMMMMMM. OM as long as you can, as loud as you can and as free as you can. You are creating a freedom space well within your maximus space of your soul. Herein lies your relic of the past that will corrugate and rectify your soul life. Here you are lighting the match to set your soul on fire and begin to breathe your soul deliverance. I am OM. OM is freedom. Freedom from all the labor you once put into living your unauthentic life. Here you are delivering your soul to a place of harmonious delight and resonance. Once you are set free, you are able to commit finally once and for all to your souls purpose.

You are heart centered and soul centered - you are cofounded by light. Here you begin your journey to pay homage to a long-lost friend, your voice. From this relation you shall endure grand exceptional spaces of love and fantastic musical harmony between souls as your soul reckoned voice shall exacerbate all others tones in order for their soul's ears to perk up and actually hear your song. Here you will begin to unilaterally exceeds others' resistance to hope and to their own versions of their own God and their own soul inside. So in doing this work, you are actuating others interpretation of their own creator and illumining the world with your song. Your song of hope is truly and utterly going to be astounding.

Just as soon as you tone up and tune up. All aspects

of the Holy Christ that are within are just waiting to be attuned to your song. Sing and sing and sing. Your song is just waiting to be heard. And by this we mean your frequency has been being attuned since the beginning of this book and so by now your resonance of light is continually being adjusted as you read each and every word of these writings. Here you will find that if you manufacture your own creativity with, you shall always manufacture your own creative without. And that is how the magic of creation happens. And the more you do for yourself, the more you can do for others, just by being the mouth piece of your God inside from what you believe to be true. Your beliefs matter and your ideas matter and your thoughts matter. This is how we are going to change the world and remediate this exist here on this planet one by one. The more we adjust our tune, the more we shall adjust society to think and feel and believe for themselves. This is key operational guidance and your hidden storage unit is full, time to move on.

Let the glory of our creator be within you in all times of song. Each word has a specific tone, be aware of your status of light. Blessed be.

Day Six • Chakra 6

Clearing our Blind Spot
The Key to our Masterpiece

    Opening or adjusting the veil of haste in order to multiplicity design our future. Here along the way of alternative guidance we find it sometimes necessary to elude our passion. However here in this space of time and space we can obliterate all aspects of self-containment and deliver upon our own self-awareness of our true bounty within. Here in this space of light or light opening diversity, we alternative seek to know and know to seek and this is our passion. Our true passion as God within is to become a full on and full-fledged bounty of might for the procession of God as an ulterior motive we counter intuitively profess to stave off all outside influences when it comes to joyous reunion with our own self-presence as we find it sometimes difficult to endure as a soul. But our bounty is such that we enjoy the happenstances of our light reunion as such and we encounter many understandable beings in our path. And in doing so we manage to forfeit the past reluctance and begin our journey home. Here we find it naturally seems to be a complete fit as we have done the past 5 arduous fleeting alignments, we have carefully and ardently given to our self a gift of admiration and fluently seek to flourish even more than at the beginning. We have found a new stepping stone so to speak and we give to our own soul presence the gift of our hearts with deep love and caring and the vocation of light, love and harmony.

As we harmoniously seek deeply inside this 6th Chakra space we indelibly find our own remedy to our own life. Here we seek to be. This keeps us confined within so that we may always see our soul and see it as a way of health and healing. We kindly give to our self so that we may kindly receive. We respectfully give to others but we cannot seem to be found in them, we can only be found within. This is we are so focused on the within here.

Now here within this 6th Chakra space we conform our seeking to a section of a real and indemnified space. We conjure up old ideas and seemingly allow them to fade. Once these old ideas are shot down, we manage to fortify our own worth as to knowing who we are and what we are seeking as we definitely know the price that we have paid. We fully understand our value of our sight as our sight is a not so foreign legion so to speak but a ramification of our old plight to be God, once again. Here in our temple lobes we fight our own heart, our own mind and our own person to seemingly try to nullify our existence of our presence of God even when we are well within the confines of our own beauty and wonder of God. Here our plight is one of intelligence, grace and unwavering knowledge of the pacifists of our own legion of self. Once we surpass this feeling of unintelligibility we shall gain certain human knowledge. This human knowledge will signify that we have crossed over from our soul space into the human space and are now living a cultural magnificent existence based upon our God centered being. Here we find it natural to simply flow and allow for these common ideas to well up and give us an idea of our new existence. By listening to these ideas which flow from within as well as without we shall endure a new way of talking, listening, feeling, and Be-ing. This is our inner guidance at long last. This is the preface in which we are to be God. Here we find it significantly well to be God inside and to formulate a new cantor of light. Here we can show up and become wealth, healing, manifestation, light, love and majesty. This is our own very well known prevalent God centered systematic pathway to the light of all things. Here in this confluence of heaven we find it finally unnecessary to have to think it all through as this is the journey of our soul's existence and here in this Chakra aligned space we give hope to our self and we give life to our souls existence.

    Now directly from this place of rest behind your eyes let's limit the satisfactory hope you have been given regarding your own wealth and its management. Here you find that you cannot be God as a source of limited ideas about you, however with regard to your space within you are God and therefore you can think God things fanatically if you will and you shall overcome all basic obstacles that show up. Now, from this place of rest behind your eyes turn your eyes inward and look back into your brain space. From this place of rest behind your eyes, begin to allow a flow to come up from the lower Chakras and flow up through each Chakra and begin to push out all unaligned ideas of who you were, and what you had become prior to now. Here your life will literally flash before your eyes. Flow the secrets, flow the lies you told yourself, flow the ideas that others kept you from achieving your goals, flow the embarrassment of how you were raised or taught or abused. Simply flow all the way up from the 1st Chakra in and through this 6th point of oblivion. Here you can begin to ascertain your human goals as a body and release them up into the universe and allow your God goals to rise up. As a once held down idea of goodness or grandeur kept hidden, begin to allow these ideas and these magical thoughts about you as a human to flow up and into your own mighty brain. Here in this leisurely God center begin to acknowledge, I am a saint, I signify grandeur. Begin to imagine all the things you would say to a queen or a king and expand your body space with this queen or king energy, you can arrange yourself to handle the flow of both. Don't be afraid allow for this grandeur to flow up and expand into your entire body space so that the flow of goodness and grandeur are so prevalent in your body that you feel you may explode with laughter. Here find your own impeachment of your old life and imagine you are stepping into the Christ castle of light and love as you are God and this is your castle and you are your own magnificence. Feel it, sit with it, vibrate it, sing it. OOOMMMMMMMMMMMM!

OM it out as sing it out to your hearts desires, I am God therefore I reside, I am God therefore I reside, I am God therefore I reside.

Really sit with this resonance of God in your castle of golden magnificence and know that you are so absolutely deserving of this space. As all of this is you, finally, at long last. You have found your own maiden voyage past your old self into a new life long adventure of faith. To you for your and by you. This has not taken so long, right? This simple source clearing of light washing deeply within the crevasses of your host body, is a small portion of what is to come. Here we find it absolutely necessary to proceed with vigor up to the next Chakra and to be entitled to greatness, grandness or magnificence. Here we find that living in this magnificence will preclude our old self from rising up. We have the magic to endure any and all capacities now. Here we seemingly are boundless and understandable. Who would think that we could do this all by ourselves and finalize our adjustment to our own civilization within. Here we are our own bounty our own light our own manna. We no longer need to seek outside to feel or to be or to know. Here we sit and contemplate only our light. This is simply the illusion we sought and now it is found deeply within. Stay with this feeling or a while.

In our 6th Chakra now, we believe that all faith is possible and we seek to know and know to seek and we feel alive here in his space behind our eyes where we can simply close our self-down and be. This is heaven, this is in a participatory a space of divine. This shall be your sought after light for your life, so be it, live it and conquer it, all other thoughts that try to nullify your extravagant existence, simply Be God. It is that simple. And as those other bounty less ideas and thoughts of, oh how can you be God? Or you have no grace, simply close your eyes turn inward and be.

Allow for this lesson to be an ongoing design for living and a spiritual routine of what is to come. From here on out you shall overcome all aspects of yourself simply by allowing in the flow of the white light and beaming it into each and every crevasse of your space so that you do not have to think about what is wrong, or why you are feeling a certain away, the light shall simply wash it all away, and as you keep this flow going, all systematic basis' will be covered and you shall simply go back to your faith in believing that all is well. All is well. And this key to your masterpiece. The more you continually seek God as your saint or savior or solution, the more you instantly remove all the old debris and begin to fully own your Be-ingness. This is key to knowledge. This is key to enlightenment and this is key to living. Life it to be lived, not endured. Life is a masterful place of non-illusory insight, here we find it impeccable to say, I in thee and thee in thou, therefore I am. Blessed be.

Day Seven • Chakra 7

Our Crown of Divinity

At the 7th Chakra, our crown divinity space is a relevant source of information. Here we find it impeccable to be on this journey home into infinity and retrieve a boundless river of information and knowledge into our God space. This is a natural flow of finesse and grandeur and as we level up to each energy body space we find it very necessary to elude the past ideas of our self as human. As we spectacularly look at our own body as energy we find it unnecessary to see the human side of us. We are no longer disillusioned by our sight of our willful body. Here we see the joy in living a God centered, God sighted and God spaced existence. Here we find it very lovely to adhere to this body of light so as to be on a course to infinity. This light passage is one of your soul's divinity at its finest and we manage to even articulate and or master our plight which at this point could be a little dismantled. We hope that you are in fine sprits as we journey on to above and beyond your past capacity to know.

As we write this together along with Andrea Elizabeth we are leisurely adhere to our stick bound guidelines by the planetary objectifiers. We have only a sound proof existence but Andrea Elizabeth can give her ideas to you just as simply as we. So here we give to you our opulent ideas of heaven as surrounded by the 7th Chakra idea of Christ and the so called following Christ Being.

The Flow of the 7th Chakra

As we flow up to our 7th Chakra and being to align with the soul of the Holy Divine both within and without and imagining a Holy white line or light in our crevasse of sight, begin to see and to align with this grand journeying figurine as a sort of magnificent 7 if you will. Allow this white light into and around your entire being.

7 New Fundamentals for Life

Here are 7 new fundamentals we wish to give each of you for your journeying.

One

Coexistence is a fraternity of Gods. Our Godlike space is one of an assortment of enlightenments and at each level we shall each find a new nirvana. In each nirvana space we shall endure a piece of heaven. And in each of these pieces of heaven we shall endure light. More fully, more opulently and more rapidly than ever before. As we sit here with you in each space of nirvana, specifically in each of your soul spaces we particularly find ways to enlighten and or endure a newness abound in each simple crevasse. We find it very unlikely that any of you have had this song sung to you before or been bequeathed a linear advancement to God or heaven. Now simply put your heart into a space of whirling light and begin to state the following notes: I in thee, I in thee, you in me, you in me, we in thee, we in thee, we in thy and we in thy. Really sound out each statement as this Holy manna is free and has been unwittingly mismanaged in previous states of body. So here we give this statement of hope and light and even forgiveness and the records all show that we have some self-hatred, or self-deception or self-something to be rid of. We believe this idea or simile alleviates most of the pain we have endured

Two

With our example of training your own willful space which has been sometimes unauthentic but we have managed to signify an elusive opening in terms of majoring in song or sound templates. The next range of sight shall become a full on gratitude game in profession of hallowed ground of perfection. Here we shall manage to interpret our song in such a fashion that Andrea Elizabeth shall perform her duties as a channeler well. Now. For the most part keep in mind that you all are in our space as we are here reading and writing this all together as a total and complete conglomeration of light. Our lights are intertwined and living as one. So as our souls match up and resonate with one another and we find that this sort of climb is very necessary to bequeath our lives and love to your soul by way of singing our systematical or even sisterly manner of the heart. Now let's endure all together this sign or signal of heart hope together as we systemically ensure this we manage to keep your space entirely in a bubble of unhindered light filled with succinct love tenderness and joy for all mankind and duly for you. As you are in this bubble of Holy light your manna shall be unearthed and your goals shall become fully interpreted by the Gods of heaven by the Gods of eternity and by the God in you. Here we intersect all aspect of Christ as God within and duly solidify ones goals as creation so here we give life to your aspect of God as we souly sing together this significance of your particular Godly light. Sit in it, feel it and join our sonnet. I find thee impeccable and I rejoice in thee. I am Holy manna from above the clouds and I souly am retrofitted unto thee. I am in the clouds I sing in the clouds and I am the clouds. I heartedly convey the lord for I am God within souly wholeheartedly and forevermore I am restored to a solemn space of Christ for I am with the living now. I live therefore I reside. I am home within my soul space of Christ. Blessed be.

Three

The third objective is to find out where aspects of our soul seep out. Our energy is a multiplicital idea of range. Here we seek to know yet we still allow parts of our soul to be mismanaged. So the third range of ideas are to seek the aspects of Christ which are thought to be safe so deeply that we sometimes miss their plight. How is it that we can know inside we carry God, but seem to forego the messages. Think of a time when we together in total concentration were given an idea of who God is. And in this time concentrate on what aspects of you kept keeping you from knowing you were God the illicit ideas of your own harrowing experiences, or the ideas from what you were called by your brothers or sisters, the bullying, etc. How did these ideas of others shape your vision of you? So here we ask that in total completeness and rhapsody and here you find it almost fanatic that you were even hindered at all. This is the multiplicity of our energy space we have such a range of ideas that were once grand yet we let others take away our grandeur based upon their ideas of who we were to them. So as we sit and admonish each and every person thoughts of us and begin to see our self through our own eyes, and through the eyes of our own God we behold a newness abound. We seek to bequeath our bounty upon our own eyes as part of the unnecessary ideas of the past. Here we seek a new sought out endeavor of faith on our part and we in the heavens conquest with and for you to be of optimum sight. As now as we give to you this bellowing sonnet we ask that you forevermore give thanks to first your bounty of Christ within and second to your past angst about you. So together now we shall sing in a bubble of glory the sight bearing presence or resonance of this Holy manna is heaven. As we sit and bequeath to us all a formidable sight of God given talent we lay this specific song out for your enjoyment. I sit and I pray and I lay my head down unto the billows of the heavenly spheres. Here I am free.

Four

This shall begin our passing of the time of how can I be myself as we shall remain seeking in this space with you. As the burrows or confines of your own sight are lifting to and from the graces of your great crevasse within, with each passing word you read the grace is flowing deeply into each light crevasse and adhering to your soul light of heaven and in each particular space we are lighting up your home within with total and complete love charity and specific reigns of gratitude, here we bring in a course for love of life. And with this course we define gratitude as a sign of heightened living or heighten being or even heightened awareness of God within. From this bountiful river of grace we portray your truest vision of God. This is your majestic bounty. This is your transparent birth unto the heaven within. There is no going up or down only inward. You are heaven and you are profound. So in this light space bubble of heaven we bring down into your crown Chakra the highest and most Holy manna given to planetary humans. The width of this immaculate light line is the exact unlimited space of your soul. Here we markup the full space value of your human soul and retrieve all that has ever tried to nullify your plight. We endeavor to flow out the old into the lower Chakras and down into mother earth herself and begin the flowing from the 7th Chakra a delightful most billowing sensation of Christ as a beam of light coming down into your crown and expanding to the width of your entire body energy space, clearing and cleaning and successfully removing any and all limited processes or ideas you have had about you and co-creating the most unlimited idea space and the most unlimited characteristics of God allowing for your soul space to be the biggest, the most billowy, the most powerful, the most essential part of you and this planet. This is where you being to flourish into the most opulent being of light the world has even known or seen. Here is your bounty. This is you. You are limitless and defined grace. This is your life option. Here you stand here you reside in your salutation of God. Blessed be.

Five

By now your body space should be full on treble. Here is a space to be worthy. Here is a space to be sound. Here is a space to be unbound from life. Here you sing without even opening your mouth, your voice is now your vibration of God. By simply Being this enhanced opulent body of light you reign. Here your vibration is literally music to ones ears and simply by being in your presence others will manage to hear their song and begin to question and begin to acknowledge themselves as Gods. This is our plight here on earth and this is why we have managed to entertain Andrea's ideas with all of your souls. As we find it very necessary to vicariously work in through and around this space as to bridge the manna back to haven as well as to earth. Your sonnet is one of beauty and can be described as delightfully progressive, so use this song you have now to bring out the light in others as they too can be and feel the God inside and they too can feel alive. All in the progression of times shall each artificial member be key. All in due time.

Six

In this 6th chain of events let's articulate a bit more on how one sees. How does one exactly go about this sight in this clearing work? We have brought out a new layer of your soul which was at first resistant. Now we do our best to match this vibration and to be illuminarily the divine truth by knowing what is well or good. The essential or universal truth is that God is. And the parts that are not of this truth can be seen for miles, and to summon out this space needs to be done invariably with one's consent. So as you read this your consent is to be a child of God in terms of your own inner soul workings. And in acknowledging this we step in and clear the way. So in a sense we are a sounding block for initiators and we bring in a higher frequency and vibratory song so that you too shall find your own truth within your own life if you wish. So our song on this part is to be one of alliance within so that you shall be of reliance without. And this shall be your duty. As we are parting ways soon the easiest thing to remember is to be God, period. That is how simple life can be. If we are being God within and true to our light, have faith in all things good we shall have a fighting chance here. Evil or bad shall pop up at times, yet it does not have to ruin our lives. We can simply stay away from the un-Godly things here on the planet and the un-Godly things that try to reign us back in as we still have some un-Godly vibrations until we fully ascertain this particular way of Be-ing. But the more we spring back into knowing we are God and climbing our way out of particular situations, the more we shall allow the new vibration to well up within our space. The more we sing, the more we vibrate and the more we live in the presence this is how we survive, this is how we shine and this is how the vibration is one of light and love and grace. We must keep this up daily in order to fully live in this capacity, this is the order of the divine

Seven

The last part is to bequeath or give unto to our soul brothers and sisters a new way of talking, walking and Be-ing. If we are flowing the white light of God in and through our Be-ing, then we begin thinking God, we begin feeling God, we begin vibrating God, we begin speaking God. As this flow continues all day every day, we are abashed from past atrocities, and we are a permissive permanent flow of the divine and our lives will begin to enact that. The more you flow the light while breathing in God and exhaling God, the more you will begin manifesting good in your life. You will imagine only God thoughts and God mannerisms and God attributes. And surely one day, you will look around at your space and see that there are only God mannerisms and God aspects in your home in your workplace in your friendships and in your relationships. And all the drama and trauma and chaos are relieved of you, simply by Be-ing God. And that is the premise of this book for you. By Be-ing God we become his Masterpiece, paint stroke by paint stroke, keystroke by keystroke thought by thought word by word action by action to simply be and live simple. Blessing to all who come to these words as the heavens are fully aware of your resonance and in each thought and mannered change you shall become a call of Christ. Blessed be. To all and many who come this way, all will be well in the manner of eternity for the universe is awaiting your words. All shall be bountiful and live in perfection

Chanting For Core Clearing

Chant For Om

- Take a deep breath in.
- As you exhale, chant the sound OM.
- When you run out of breath, breathe in, and repeat the chant.
- Continue at your own pace for 2 to 3 minutes.
- I suggest OM-ing at each Chakra space.

Chant For A-U-M

- Take a deep breath in
- As you exhale, in the same breath chant Aaa Uuu-Mmm
- Feel the "Aaa" sound in your belly, "Uuu" in your chest area, and "Mmm" in your head
- Breathe in again and continue at your own pace for 2-3 minutes I suggest AUM-ing at each Chakra space

As you chant, you raise the vibration of the whole physiology of your body space. Whenever you chant, chant fully. Open your heart, open your throat, open each Chakra space and chant with your whole body; lose yourself to the chant. Ultimately you are chanting to our own soul—the divinity within you

Rumi said, "I want to sing like the birds, not caring who listens or what they think."

This is how you should chant.

Toning For Core Clearing

As everything in the universe is sound or vibration, a disharmony in one of those sounds or a break in the unfolding of the sequence of sounds, leads to discomfort, disease, and a loss of wholeness. As an example, if one musician in an orchestra is playing off key, there is a loss of harmony in the whole piece of music. You can correct that by having a second musician stand next to the first one and play the correct notes. Just by hearing the correct notes, the first musician will automatically begin playing correctly.

Similarly, if there is a disharmony in your physiology, and you know the correct vibration for that area, you can begin to correct the imbalance by chanting or toning that sound. For example, if you have a problem with your eyes, and you know the sound relating to the eyes, you can activate the healing process for that area by chanting that sound (silently or aloud) and directing the vibration into the area of the eyes. I include these Examples of Toning Sounds for the Body.

NOTE: The vowel sounds AHAA, EEE, EYE, OOO, UUU are non-local or non-specific. If you don't know the sound for an area of the body, you can chant any of the vowel sounds and direct its vibration into that area.

NNN	Ears
EEMM	Eyes
LMM	Nose
MMM	Sinuses
PAAM	Stomach
KAA GAA GHA	Throat
MAM	Reproductive Organs
MM-EE-AH-UU	Relaxing, Bedtime
SSSS	Lungs and Large Intestine
SHHH	Liver and Small Intestine
WOOO	Kidneys and Bladder
MA	Heart
HAA	Diaphram
YAA YU YI	Jaw
UU-AH-EE-MM	Energizing, Wakeup

Core Cleansing Chakra Chants

When a Chakra or energy center is closed off or dislodged by feelings or emotions, there is an infinite rise in non-clarity within. You may be feeling a general malaise or just plain sadness. Opening up all energetic body centers can and will allow for the flow of the universal life energy to ground and center your being. Using the Chakra Chants as a harmonious version of the Holy Christ Being-ness you can begin to give rise to the nature of your body's intelligence. By allowing this intelligence to speak and demand wholeness within you can envision a new way of living and a new way of cadence within.

Here your Holy mantra of non-division or precise living is sound and effective. A new vision for your eternity can begin to take shape and a new version of you as God can ruminate wholeness by and through your endeavor to wholeness. All has taken place at the precise time as directed by you.

Peace unto thee, until we meet and vibrate as one once again on our journey. Blessed be.

CHAKRA	CHANT
1st Chakra, base of the spine	LAAM
2nd Chakra, sacral area	VAAM
3rd Chakra, navel area	RAAM
4th Chakra, heart area	YAAM
5th Chakra, throat area	HAAM
6th Chakra, between eyebrow	AUM
7th Chakra, crown (top) of head	SO-HAM

Sounds Of Love

Core Cleansing Chakra

The 7 Chakra Sounds of Love

As an added bonus I include the Seven Sounds of love from the Indian Sanskrit Mantric Sounds.

Each Sound of Love I believe is based upon our bounty of the past illusion of haste. To begin settling down our soul to such an intrepid space of silence is key to breaking our illusion of having to always be moving and achieving something outside of our self. Self enhancement is such an inside job that so many seemingly miss the advantages of sitting and Be-ing Love. Perhaps this exercise may bring you back to the non-illusory space where you decide the unimaginable of Home is where Love resides and God is key. Here I believe this all to be a true statement as your Bounty of Love lies within. Your key to a bountiful life begins where the heart lies within and at the point of solemn peace.

Blessed be.

Use each sound as a remnant of holiness, love and peace. Begin to follow as each sound begins at the hallowedness of Christ. Love is key to manifesting. Manifesting is key to loving. Loving is key to forgiveness. Blessed be.

1st Chakra	Root	SA
2nd Chakra	Sacral	RE
3rd Chakra	Solar Plexus	GA
4th Chakra	Heart	MA
5th Chakra	Throat	PA
6th Chakra	3rd Eye	DHA
Back of Head		NI
7th Chakra	Crown	SA

Becoming God By Design

As this book comes to an end and you can finally decide for yourself who God really is or is not, I believe that during the concourse of your awakening life, you can begin to demolish your past ideas and create or co-create a new version of your own Holiness deep inside. There are no future characatures coming to save us, we are it. We are our own saviors. We are our own God by Design.

You get to choose what that looks like. Your Design. Your comingling. Your choice. You decide. Period. That is what your God looks like. Your God looks like you. That is why I had to portray this version of somewhat terse words in order to get your attention. This is not some immaculatory intervention, this is an original version of you as God, by design. You are the Designer and you can now, from this point forward create a new version of you for your life and begin to determine just how you want to create a space for this design in your life. How shall you portray this new found God to the world. How shall you feed it? How shall you clothe it? How shall you house it? This is an entirely new version of you. Therefore, how shall you design a new life for you? What shall be the new results for living this bountiful existence? What shall be its value to you? How shall you afford this new Being? How shall you operate this new vehicle? All good questions. But alas you have your own fervor or passion, your own intuition to work from. This allowing business is one of grandness and fortune. Who is to say that you are not great or fortunate. Not one person, as that old illusion of searching outside yourself is gone, and you shall now only have to search within. And finding the truths about you which is that your truth, is your truth. Nothing less, nothing more. You are God. End of story. God is the answer. What is the question? Blessed be!

Ending words

As a spiritual channel, I am able to receive transmissions from all over the planet. The more places I visit, the more chatty Mother Earth becomes. My writings are meant to be in the way of conversations. Conversations with Mother Earth, Spirit, The Ascended Masters, Guides, Past Relics, you name it. Each aspect of time is of no measure to me as I am able to fully tap into and allow the Universe to speak. I honestly have no choice but to write as none of these sensational beings will not let up until I do. If these readings are a bit non-distinguishable at first, keep reading, you will truly catch on. These writings are in the form of healing, mainly. Each and every book I write has a main goal, and that main goal is to teach that we Are God Within. And to stop seeking accomplishment on the outside, but to truly master our own self on the inside. Each true aspect of self has a monetary vibration of the literal heavens, and this what my primary focus of this book, to become God's Masterpiece.

Blessed Be to All!
In deep appreciation and light,

Andrea Elizabeth

www.ingramcontent.com/pod-product-compliance
Lightning Source LLC
Chambersburg PA
CBHW071025080526
44587CB00015B/2506